AUSTERITY BUSINESS

AUSTERITY BUSINESS

39 Tips for Doing More with Less

ALEX PRATT

A John Wiley and Sons, Ltd, Publication

This edition first published by John Wiley & Sons Ltd in 2010
Copyright © 2010 Alex Pratt

Registered office
John Wiley & Sons Ltd, The Atrium, Southern Gate, Chichester, West Sussex,
PO19 8SQ, United Kingdom

For details of our global editorial offices, for customer services and for information
about how to apply for permission to reuse the copyright material in this book please
see our website at www.wiley.com

ISBN 978-0-470-68872-4

A catalogue record for this book is available from the British Library.

Set in 11.5/17 pt Jenson Pro by Sparks – www.sparkspublishing.com
Printed in Great Britain by TJ International Ltd, Padstow, Cornwall

CONTENTS

ABOUT THE AUTHOR

Alex Pratt is an award-winning entrepreneur and one of the UK's leading business figures. He started trading bankrupt stock at the age of 16, and was quickly spotted as a national rising business star.

Today, Alex is Director of Serious Brands. He has worked with several governments as an advisor on business, competitiveness and innovation. He is also actively involved in setting up the UK's National Enterprise Academy.

www.alexpratt.co.uk

ACKNOWLEDGEMENTS

To everyone who helped me along the way, especially my dad, thank you. I'm also indebted to Ellen Hallsworth who helped me craft coherent tips from my rambling thoughts.

INTRODUCTION

A couple of years ago, the world was hit by a global economic pandemic. Titanic companies that seemed 'too big to fail' found out they were also too big to fit the lifeboats. General Motors became the biggest bankruptcy of all time. The collapse of Lehman Brothers sparked a global financial meltdown on a scale not seen since the Great Depression. Iceland (the country) went bust. Oops.

It seems like nobody on the planet was untouched by this economic crisis. Healthy, productive businesses were laid low in a heartbeat, and much lauded business models now appear in retrospect to have been led by the highly paid deaf, dumb and blind. Mind you, hindsight is a wonderful thing. Who could have predicted that the mighty German economy would have come to be seen as weak because of its dependence on strong export performance? And who would have thought that City bankers, once praised as heroes for making us all richer, would become public enemy number one in such a short space of time?

Today, we're all living with the consequences and picking up the pieces. Much of what we took as certain a short time ago has evaporated. One thing is certain, running or managing a business is now a fundamentally different challenge. This feels like Business 2.0, and it seems a lot of the rules have changed.

FROM HERE TO AUSTERITY

So what exactly has changed? World trade paused and took a deep breath when the credit crunch landed. An initial whirlwind in the financial markets triggered an earthquake in construction and a drought in liquidity, which in turn went on to feed a tsunami of unemployment. Throw in the rapidly ageing populations in the developed economies, levels of public and private national debt not seen in the West outside of World Wars, and a global banking system on its knees. Then there is the rapid and unprecedented shift of economic power from West to East, away from traditional western democracies to more autocratic trading zones like China, Russia and the Middle East. And don't forget the expected shortages in energy, food and water fed by dwindling stocks of natural resources and a burgeoning global population. This will all have a profound effect on how business gets done. Take nothing for granted.

The combination of the credit crunch and a global recession has cleared the mist that was covering the harsh economic truth that we live in a world of scarce resources. It now seems clear that we've already moved from the age of plenty into a new era of austerity. We need to get to grips with a number of new realities. Did you think you knew about how to win business, how to service customers and where cash comes from? Think again.

Pre-crisis demand was fashion-driven, fed by western consumers who were making businesses rich and driving forward the forces of globalisation. We found we could always spend a bit more, take that extra business trip and afford that pay rise to our top performers, because insatiable consumers, especially the baby boomer generation, were always going to want more tomorrow than they consumed today. Only a couple of years ago, staff retention had gone all power naps and duvet days. It would have been inconceivable to approach a dedicated team with a pay cut proposal, yet global airlines, international phone companies and worldwide management consultancies have now all had to put this to the test. Some have moved flexibly and nimbly in the right direction to occupy a new trading space. Others have become mired in the inertia of legacy systems and thinking, or frozen rigid in pure panic.

Now, shocked by the fact that living standards don't just keep getting higher and higher, buyers are focusing more on what they need, less on what they fancy and much less on what the neighbours think. The disposable desires of recent generations are already being replaced by more of a 'make do and mend' mentality.

Customers have changed, and as businesses, we need to change with them.

Steady on, you might think. The markets are looking up, and conditions might well return back to normal soon. Sadly not. The financial crisis is actually the least of our worries. Add in the other long term austerity drivers, such as the fiscal debt, unsustainable usage of natural resources and the ageing workforce, and the conditions for permanent change and more austere times for the West look clear.

Of course, changing the habits of bloated businesses and consumers is more easily said than done. While austerity conditions will need hungry, more focused business minds, not every business decision maker will turn the changes to their advantage by switching early enough to new thriftier winning ways. Like the mice in *Who Moved My Cheese*, many will be paralysed and will struggle to live beyond their previous comforts.

There will be no return to normality. It's time to wake up and smell the austerity.

HOW THIS BOOK HELPS

Far too often, business books look in the rear-view mirror. There are basically three types, and all are limited in the help they can offer you, as an entrepreneur or manager, in coping with the new world of austerity.

This book could have given you my '10 simple rules for guaranteed business success' – the problem is, I don't know them. They don't really exist. Of course I know that 'cash is king', 'pricing is pivotal' and 'people make the difference'. But, if you're reading this book, you already know that too. We also know that what works for you is probably not right for me, so we may as well be honest with each other and state upfront that there are no simple universal business rules.

Then there's the 'Do it my way. Look, it worked for me!' type of business book. But this is just as flawed as an aid to your own success. Sure, these stories are interesting for the great job they do in highlighting that successful entrepreneurs are as fallible as the rest of us. But other than reinforcing the critical roles played by courage, hard work and luck in attaining success in the first place, they fall short of arming us with practical new habits and thinking. Your journey is your own, pure and simple.

Finally, you get the dried and dusted academic kind of business book. 'We looked at 500 firms, and this is what we found'. This kind of book is less about ego; it's founded on evidence, methodology and analysis. The post-hoc rationalisation of the past does create some wonderfully intricate and complicated mappings of what it took to succeed. Life is indeed very complex, but I'm not sure it needs to be quite as complicated as we sometimes like to make it appear.

That's why I've tried to make this book different. The age of austerity business is all about boldly going where your business has not gone before. The authors of the next successful entrepreneur autobiographies will be those who are today focused on mastering what they do, on building confidence and the courage to do more of it, and on quickly adopting changing habits fit for winning ways in the face of a rapidly changing world. There is no roadmap to copy.

I've been working at the coalface of business since I first began trading bankrupt stock, aged sixteen. I haven't gone flat out to make a massive pile yet, and I don't presume to tell you that I know better than you. Like you, I'm still learning, and this period of austerity has been a huge shock for me too. What I have done is dedicate myself to running the most interesting small business I can, and this book seeks to share some of that with you. I can point you to some key questions and tips, suggest implications and help you to conclusions, but you will need to come to your own truths and answers. Doffing my hat to a previous period of austerity, I've collected my thoughts into 'the 39 tips' and hope that at least some of them will strike a chord with you and make a difference to your prospects. I've divided these into the four areas that I've found are crucial for any business to get straight: attitude; people; customers and strategy. In each section, I've included a range of thoughts, suggestions and ideas, ranging from those which could have an immediate impact on your bottom line, to the small things that can make a big difference.

Try to see this as a joint adventure in this new age of austerity, where no-one really knows what's going to happen. There is unlikely to be another moment so rich in business opportunity in our lifetimes, and I truly hope you'll come to your new business truths and decisions much faster having read this book. Grab your chances and adapt in real time.

Business is easy. If only the world would stand still.

PART I

ATTITUDE

TIP 1

FACE THE TRUTH

A lie would have no sense unless the truth were felt to be dangerous.

Alfred Adler

No-one has lived through such a fundamental moment of change in the world of business. Not you, not your boss, not your employees. Not even me. The old period of plenty is dead. A sustained era of austerity is upon us.

No wonder you bought this book.

Looking at the world around you, with rising unemployment, massive debts, grim GDP figures and global warming rising up the agenda, and worries about cuts and inflation lying ahead, the words of the old Beatles' song comes to mind – 'Yesterday, all my troubles seemed so far away'. But that was then, yesterday. This is now. The question here is: do you still believe in yesterday? Even more worryingly: are you still doing business like it is yesterday?

We have hit a massively disruptive moment – the global credit crunch. You may well feel like one of those old-fashioned cartoon characters, whose legs keep spinning faster and faster in an attempt to stay airborne after running over the edge of a cliff. I know I sometimes do. A couple of years ago, I had a plan for 70% growth, which turned into 10% shrinkage. As an entrepreneur, I've therefore spent much of the year braced in the crash position, waiting to re-establish contact with terra firma. Well, the news is that the landscape at the bottom of the cliff is very different from how things looked at the top.

For a long time, some people continued to believe that the world was flat, that men would never fly and that there would never be a market for handheld music devices. Now, received economic wisdom has also taken a beating from the truth.

You might, however, be forgiven for assuming that, even at the dawn of this new age of austerity, where we're all going to have to do much more with much less, you'll just adapt anyway. After all, you're a winner. Chances are you're going to be able to self-adjust and make the most of it. Of course, this might well be true, but do you really want to bet the farm on your pride, or is it better to swallow it this time?

Coming to a decision is the easy part. But if you're an analogue entrepreneur in a digital world where we're heading for switch off, I've got news for you, it's taking action that's the hard part. It's living out the necessary new habits, day after day, week after week, which is such a tough call. I can't tell you how often I've decided to become thinner, but despite that, after years and years of trying, I still eat chocolate when I'm feeling tired and low. Do you think I'm thin? Exactly.

In business, as in life, old habits die a slow death, especially those that may have worked well for you in the past. We need to work seriously hard to kill them off.

Adjust your set for the age of austerity.

As a quick experiment, if you want to be reminded of how hard it is to change ingrained habits, take up the simple challenge of wearing your watch on the other wrist for a day. No, seriously. Stop reading for a moment, switch your watch to the other wrist, and only then read on.

I bet it's already annoying you. Notice how tricky it was to put the watch on in the first place. You're probably itching to put it back on the other wrist, where it belongs, because it feels so heavy and so discombobulating.

What's the time? Did you reach for the old wrist first? See what I mean? Even for a stupid book experiment, changing the habits of a lifetime is a pretty tough ask. What if your very survival depends on it?

During the times of plenty, entrepreneurs and business leaders were pretty much all in the habit of focusing on the pursuit of growth, of market share, of dominating a particular market space. Asked the question 'how big is your company?' like many business people, I've always been used to answering by spouting our turnover figures, or how many employees we have. Rarely did I stop to mention the net profit. Never would I have stopped to add in the details of our cash-flow. Bigger, in terms of the headline figures, was simply better.

In the past couple of years, however, as the new austerity has emerged, we have all come to know stories of the businesses that went bust because they, astonishingly, never made a profit. By gorging on more and more cheap debt, they managed to grow their turnover, increase staff numbers, and lease swankier offices, *without ever making any real money*. We've also all got used to the stories of otherwise perfectly sound businesses which became so used to times of plenty, that they didn't believe the age-old mantra 'cash is king' and forgot that they had to guard against not having enough money in the bank to pay the bills. It was the very same hubris and obsession with growth that led to the dot com boom and bust at the start of this millennium. When will we ever learn?

Austerity must offer a better way.

Do you still think that chasing turnover is the right way to measure success? Wouldn't the efficiency with which you put your cash to use be a better way to look at things? Do you still measure your success as a leader by the size of the team you manage, or by how much you improved the balance sheet? Would you ever walk away from an unprofitable customer who was waving money at you? Get real.

To many people ingrained in the ways of modern business, these behaviours may well seem a little old-fashioned. They are. They're the basics, the foundations of every business success. Get to know and like them again.

TIP 2

GIRAFFES DON'T JUMP

*There are no constraints on the human mind,
no walls around the human spirit, no barriers
to our progress except those we ourselves erect.*

Ronald Reagan

N ow, you're almost certainly wondering what on earth a giraffe could teach you about managing and growing a business through the age of austerity. Read on …

It's pretty common knowledge that giraffes are the world's tallest animals, and that they have the longest legs of any animal in the world too. What you might not have known is that giraffes sleep and give birth standing up. In fact, they do most things standing up, but it's the point about giving birth that's of most interest to us. What it means is that a baby giraffe emerges onto the planet and is immediately faced with a six foot drop, and is almost certainly dropped on its head.

At first, the experience might not seem to bother the giraffe too much – but it has an immense impact in later life. Throughout their twenty-odd year lifespan, *giraffes don't jump*. Never. Paradoxically, the world's tallest animal is actually scared of heights. You can see this phenomenon in action in any zoo, anywhere in the world. You might expect a large animal like a giraffe to be penned in by high electric fences, but instead there are often just low barriers and narrow moats separating them from the general public. Every giraffe is physically capable of jumping the moat and fence combination, but none ever does. That first terrifying bump on the head mentally conditions the giraffe into the firm impression that it's better off with four feet firmly on the ground.

The point of all this is that as managers, entrepreneurs and employees we're all far guiltier than we might think of behaving like giraffes. We too are conditioned far more than we think by our earlier experiences and how we interpret them. This may be limiting enough most of the time, but when recession and austerity strike, it's downright dangerous. Just when we need to change most, we may well find that we can't. We too can be hemmed in by our past, our subconscious fears, our psychological conditioning or simply by the idea that we've always done it that way. Comfort and fear can be killers.

I was built by a British working class family in the 1970s. This conditioning equipped me for such wonderful things as discos, big hair and Kojak. I was built to take off, dry and refit a damp distributor cap. Built to never waste a penny. Built to lick my plate clean. This was the era of the Apollo Moon landings, Mohammed Ali and The Sex Pistols. All of this suggested that anything was possible, if only you worked hard enough.

Like many others of my generation, as time has gone on, I've succeeded sometimes by relying heavily on this early conditioning, and sometimes by working hard to overcome it. Some of these values, particularly frugality, are worth revisiting in the era of austerity business – there is a lot that we can learn from the past. Yet in other ways, the world has moved on so much further and faster than we have ourselves. Who could have predicted that a kid who grew up in a world where telephones were just about as rare as private planes, would now live surrounded by internet-enabled wireless laptops, iPods and 3G mobile BlackBerries with GPS, texting and international roaming?

More recently, we've been conditioned to accept limitless growth as the norm, readily available debt being proffered to us on every corner, the nice decade. For anyone, like me, who's grown used to doing business in such an environment, that too forms part of our conditioning from which we now need to break free.

We're generally good at accepting and slowly adapting to gradual change over time. Of course we are, otherwise we'd still be listening to cassette tapes, sitting at our desks in flared trousers, and walking over to have a look at the telex machine. Few people would volunteer to go back in time to visit a dentist or buy a computer, after all. But sometimes we need more than gradual change.

To survive in the world of austerity business, you must escape your inner giraffe.

What makes humans different from giraffes is the fact that we're constantly putting different spins on our experiences. Two people, faced with the same events and with the same conditioning, can still react entirely differently. This is our 'get out of jail free' card, if only we know when and how to use it. Unlike giraffes, most humans would eventually find a way of jumping the moat to escape their enclosure if it caught fire. If you hadn't already realised, this is more or less what's happened ... the world you once knew is in flames.

I'm not your therapist, but I would like to offer you a few ways to overcome yourself in the drive for success in changing economic times. Just because you bumped your head at the end of the noughties, doesn't mean you can't jump into austerity. The fact that your first presentation sucked doesn't mean that you have to be petrified every time you stand in front of a crowd. Many of our business challenges are won or lost inside our heads.

To survive in the brave new era of austerity, you must work in the world as it really is, rather than living imprisoned by yesterday's truths and assumptions.

TIP 3

ADJUST YOUR SET

We must adjust to changing times and still hold to unchanging principles.

Jimmy Carter

When I was a lad, we would sometimes get temporary reception glitches on our TV, normally accompanied by a message to sit tight and be patient. 'Do not adjust your set' the BBC voice would boom, in Queen's English. Normal service, we were informed, would soon be resumed.

We are now living through just such a glitch in the global economy. More dollars have been written off than you or I could even begin to write down. In the UK alone, the economy contracted by over 6% in a year, which is comparable to the fall during the Great Depression. The scale and speed of this contraction makes it worse than anything we have ever known. Massive economic wipeouts don't right themselves quickly. Do you really believe that normal service will soon be resumed?

We've just lived through a period in which capitalism has been through unprecedented turmoil. It's time to adjust your set.

Just to recap, in the UK, as in most other countries in the West, in the past couple of years it seems that we have only narrowly avoided the prospect of economic Armageddon. The commanding heights of the global banking system were nationalised by governments now overburdened by the colossal amounts of public debt they must carry. Put bluntly, we face years of economic misery, and a long, slow and painful recovery. We are held back by sky-high levels of public and private debt, the inevitable tightening of regulation after the subprime horse has bolted, and by the demographic and pensions time-bomb which mean that already, in the UK, we have more people aged over 60 than under 15. This is pretty scary stuff.

Austerity now seems inevitable. Businesses are going to have to do something pretty amazing to grow with less labour and less capital at their disposal. To pay off our debts and maintain our living standards, we're going to have to do a lot more with a lot less. Consumers are going to be very risk-averse, and very savvy about how and where they spend their money. Public spending is likely to be cut drastically, and strikes and stoppages will almost certainly follow. There are going to be a lot more rules. Many employees may have to be prepared to accept less if it means keeping their jobs. Borrowing will no longer be a human right, as lenders remember that they need to make a margin and get their money back. Oil, food and water are going to be in short supply. Global power is going to shift from the creaky and indebted old economies of the West to the new ones in the East, rich in sovereign wealth and young talent.

The tightening of economic conditions is going to make business a whole different ballgame.

But it's not all doom and gloom. On the plus side, austerity conditions will bring about a period of frugality that will push us into being less complacent about our prosperity. Austerity will make us hungry enough to be as bold as we need to be to win in the gladiatorial contest that is modern business. Austerity will mean that talent, space and money all become cheaper than before. You will find that your suppliers are more negotiable than they used to be, and you will also need to show more flexibility. Disruptive moments always hold rich pickings for start-ups and innovators. Some of today's biggest brands all got going during tough times. Frugality breeds self-discipline and efficiency.

Make no mistake, though, we face an era of business as *unusual*. I'm taking the view that not only do I need to adjust my set, I need to go the whole hog and upgrade my cruddy old analogue set for some high-definition digital equipment. This may not appear very austere at first sight. Think about it though – with a digital TV you get a much clearer picture, something we will all need in uncertain austere business conditions.

TIP 4

OPPORTUNITIES DON'T KNOCK

There is a tide in the affairs of men,
Which, taken at the flood, leads on to fortune.

William Shakespeare

Opportunity is an interesting word. For most entrepreneurs in particular, it's what gets them up in the morning. But what do you do when opportunities don't come knocking?

It helps to know the word 'opportunity' comes from the Latin *ob portu* which was the phrase used for boats laying up off-shore in the days before ports had been built. The boats would sit out in the bay, waiting for the tide to turn, to ride it into shore to offload their cargo.

You see, the very word opportunity itself is based on the idea that good fortune comes in waves. It's a pretty good metaphor for running a business in blustery economic conditions. Successful businesses surf the waves of change. The stormy economic seas around us have brought a wealth of opportunities and threats. There's more of everything: more fear, more barriers to success, more demands on every bit of your business, but also, crucially, more chance of renewal. Don't overplay the threats and end up ignoring the flood of opportunities.

In trying to navigate these treacherous economic seas, many of your competitors will sink without trace. Many others will batten down the hatches and stay below deck to sit out the rough weather. Not you. To do more than just survive the age of austerity, you're going to have to get out there, lash yourself to the deck and scan the horizon, looking for those new chances to sail to shore safely, picking up new customers along the way. Trust me, in times of austerity, customers just don't swim out to greet you in the bay.

The difference between truly great and very average companies is often how far they're willing to go to find this kind of opportunity. If you'll go out on a limb and spend, spend, spend on advertising just when conditions seem at their toughest, it's a risky strategy, it may even seem at odds with a policy of austerity, but done well it will set you apart. If you're bold enough to take your sector by surprise, to be really determined and hungry to win, then you're likely to keep sailing on through the storm.

Think of all those great companies which were born into economic squalls in the first place. Did you know that Disney, HP, Google, Burger King, and FedEx all started when times were tough? My guess is that if you're smart enough to spot big opportunities in a recession, and brave enough to ride out the storm, you're pretty damn smart and brave, and that's going to pay off when times get better.

In all my years in business, I've come to the conclusion that it's how you respond to opportunities, and how you go out and find them, that separates winners from wannabes. Which are you? How are you going to prove it tomorrow?

TIP 5

YOUR FIVE A DAY

New opinions often appear first as jokes, then as blasphemies and treason, then as questions open to discussion, and finally as established truths.

George Bernard Shaw

I n these tips and thoughts on doing more with less, on making do with the global economy and mending your own business, I really want to avoid the tired old platitudes about business success. I've read more than my fair share of business books in my time, and it's always struck me as a bit of an insult to our intelligence to tell us that we need to work hard, make sacrifices and be determined to succeed in business. What do they think we are doing?! Kicking back with a cold beer and chilling on the beach?

It's a competition. If you're not a winner, you're a loser. If you're not staying with the times, you're falling behind. If you're not adapting to change, you are a victim of it. In business, spotting change, planning it, pontificating about it and discussing it counts for nothing unless you take action. This may sound harsh, but it's worth reminding ourselves just how tough it now is out there. Nobody ever said austerity was going to be easy.

Anyway, trying to avoid platitudes, I want to give you a few questions which may help you to convert thought into action. From my own life at the coalface, running a business, I know they've often helped me to take the small, but sometimes significant, steps that have made a difference to the way I do things. I hope they'll work just as well for you too.

The government tells us that for our health and wellbeing, we should take our 'five a day' – five portions of fruit and vegetables as part of our daily diet. I can't say I always manage that, but here are my five a day for business wellbeing.

1 AM I IN DENIAL?

When you wake up, there can be a temptation to pull the duvet back over your head when times are tough, to switch off to the world outside, in the hope that when you come up for air everything will be reassuringly back to normal. Think about it though. It didn't work for the dinosaurs. It certainly hasn't worked for the British motor industry. Realistically, it won't work for you either.

This is not an austerity breeze just blowing through. We all face the denial stage, but those who profit most from change find ways to pick themselves up and dust themselves off faster than the rest of the pack. This would be a great moment to get over yourself.

2 IS MY GLASS HALF FULL?

We entrepreneurial types are generally an optimistic bunch. We tend to see the opportunity in any moment, well before the accompanying risks emerge over the horizon. In the course of day to day work, we like to see chances, not chores, pleasure, not pain, more 'get to dos' than 'got to dos'.

Pessimists, on the other hand, see the missing thimble in a pint glass and can find plenty to complain about at the best of times. For a pessimist, surrounded by 'can't doers' the prospect of change will loom very large, prompting either panic or resignation. Neither of these responses is going to help.

It's staying purposeful, refining what we are good at and playing to our strengths that build our sustainable competitive advantage. Accentuate the positive. And remember, there's no shame in a laugh.

(3)   AM I OPEN AND TRANSPARENT?

It's people who drive the profits that most businesses make. Talent, by its very nature is not stupid. The best people in any company will sniff out fear and indecision, and will spot insincerity, no matter how well-camouflaged you think it is. The only way to stop fear from becoming paralysis, is to be upfront and open.

The best leaders foster their followers. They do this by being transparent, communicating well, showing humility and cheerfully admitting what they don't know. They have a strong story that lights a fire in the bellies of those they work with.

What news are you going to share today?

(4) DO I BELIEVE IN FACT OR FICTION?

Ignorance may be bliss elsewhere in life, but in business, fresh solid data is vital. We can all busk it in the good times, but knowing and watching the numbers is a matter of life or death when every penny counts.

Keep your eye on the cash, get your bank on side and keep it there, de-bloat your stock and make sure that there's no weakest link in your supply chain. Use the numbers to face the truth, and revisit every element of the business model and every process to make it fit that new reality. Now is a good time to redesign the dashboard by which you drive the business.

(5) AM I PANICKING OR FOCUSING?

Business has always been a bit of a rollercoaster. It's just that now the drop is even more intense and adrenaline soaked than you ever expected. The only question remaining is whether you scream, shut your eyes and hold on for dear life, or relax and enjoy the ride.

Don't rely on any knee-jerk reactions in the panic of the moment. Make sure that, however out of your depth you feel, you're always waving, not drowning.

NO ENTREPRENEUR IS AN ISLAND

Nothing ever exists entirely alone; everything is in relation to everything else.

Buddha

The great English poet John Donne once famously wrote: 'No man is an island'.

If you're an entrepreneur or business leader, whether you're a man or a woman, a truer word was never spoken.

We all know by now that you can't get anything done alone, that you need to build, work with and motivate a team to make things happen. When the going gets tough, I'm sure you'll find that this perennial management truth becomes crystal clear. It's a rare business that does not rely on a team somewhere along the line.

Like you, the team around you is likely to suffer from old habits, formed in an age of plenty. In the mission-speak of management gurus and HR directors, you might describe this as your 'culture'. This is how things actually get done around the place. As Aristotle reminded us 'we are what we repeatedly do'.

In different companies, different cultures operate. Some places, people never talk to each other unless they can possibly help it. In other offices, it's the norm that you'll stay late, and always go the extra mile. In some places, the British parliament to name one example, it's the norm to fiddle your expenses. The underlying team culture forms various, well-trodden paths, good and bad, that affect every aspect of your business, from how you handle customer complaints, to how you approach new product development and how you deal with your debtor book.

All this stuff about culture and teams is important to understand because getting your business ready for the age of austerity, and replacing old habits with new ones, is at least as much about the processes deployed to change how things are done, as it is about the sheer willpower to change them in the first place. Changing the way that the people around you behave, and the way that they see things, is an enormous leadership challenge.

If you thought leading a team was testing in the good times, honestly, you ain't seen nothing yet. When the people around you are worried and overworked, they will find it harder than ever to believe that you know any more than they do. Bring your core team together quickly, tell them what you know and what you don't, as well as what you believe is the best way to get through this. If you are to adopt the radically new approach that austerity demands, every manager in the business will need to act as a disciple, explaining what this new approach means for everyone else in the business, in terms they will understand.

Of course, tough times can embitter people as well as empowering them. Make no mistake, though, times of austerity leave absolutely no room for office politics and power games. Everyone says they hate them, but most people still play them. In the good times you may well have tolerated the inefficiencies of squabbling and silo working. It's in the really tough times that your team has to be just that – a team.

Any team, and therefore any enterprise, wins or loses on the combination of the habits, standards and patterns by which it lives and operates, plus the talent and determination with which these attributes are executed in the field of play. An average team doing the right things will always outperform talent headed in the wrong direction. That's why, in the fallout of global financial crisis, many of the seemingly boring businesses that form the backbone of our economy and our day to day lives continue to survive and even thrive. Meanwhile, the top talent at banks, people with PhDs in astrophysics, whose special knowledge and powers meant that even their bosses didn't understand what they were doing, while they needed trucks to drive their bonuses home, led the world into a colossal crisis.

Pulling together and making common sense common practice is the really smart thing to do. If such a major, shared crisis and challenge doesn't invoke a bit of Dunkirk spirit and pull your team together like never before, then what will?

That should be your real business plan.

TIP 7

DON'T PUT OFF 'TIL TOMORROW WHAT YOU CAN DO TODAY

Procrastination is opportunity's natural assassin.

Victor Kiam

Too often, when we face difficulties ahead, we are caught like rabbits, staring into the headlights of oncoming disaster.

Don't do this. Sitting there staring, dazzled by your problems, won't change anything.

Doing business in austerity conditions will mean you're going to be confronted with some pretty tough decisions. Your nerves will be tested. The way you respond to these challenges will shape your chances of thriving or diving.

If you think about it, if you're doing something wrong, the longer you leave it to put it right, the more it is going to cost you. Likewise, if you're missing out on doing something big, the sooner you do it, the sooner you'll gain the potential benefits. Make those inconvenient phone calls now, not tomorrow. When you spot a leak, fix it. Don't give weak performers endless chances to hit the mark. I know that I'm bad at saying 'no' – I'll put things off and off to avoid doing it. But the only way to get better at saying 'no' is to get more practice.

Austerity conditions are, in many ways, just like battle conditions. Imagine your platoon is on the run, looking all the time to take new ground. If you run at the pace of the slowest, or give yourself too much of a break, you stand to lose out big time. You can't sit there contemplatively, weighing up all the options, when shrapnel is flying in your face. You must act without delay.

Being brilliant at deciding takes courage. Take any cloth-cutting decisions early, and say 'No' more often. Your business needs it.

TIP 8

TIME POVERTY

The only reason for time is that everything doesn't happen at once.

Albert Einstein

When did you last say: 'I just don't have time'? Pleading time poverty is almost a badge of honour in today's overworked world.

Well, guess what? There's just as much time today as there was yesterday. One thing that austerity most definitely does not change is the amount of time available in a day. Twenty-four hours of it. Time makes us all equal too – whether you've been buffeted by the downturn or come out on top, you'll have exactly as much time as the next guy.

What does change, though (which is why I'm raising it) is our attitude to time, and the value we each place on it. If we're feeling stretched financially, we'll value time less and extra money in our pockets much, much more. We'll drive further to get to a cheaper supermarket and queue there for longer, thinking so hard about the bargains in the trolley that we don't complain. We'll buy cheaper, flatpack furniture and build it ourselves. To win from this change, think hard about what it means for you. Could you give your customers more value by taking up a bit more of their time?

When you find yourself pleading time poverty, and saying you're just far too busy, stop and think about it. People who do this create an image of themselves as out of their depth, insecure and unable to cope. More than ever, in these times of austerity, think how much better it is to be the person who takes everything thrown at them in their stride, who just gets the work done.

You could fill acres of shelf space with all the books that have been written about time management, so the last thing I'd want to do is to add to that. In fact, I believe the very idea of time management is a complete misnomer. It treats time as if it were a resource which you can own, save and spend. It isn't. Time doesn't really exist, and we definitely can't control it. It just is. The only choice that you have is whether you are 'all there' in every single moment of time, making the most of it, or not. You are unable to change the past, but you can ruin the present by worrying about the future. Today is the tomorrow you worried about yesterday. Concentrate on today. It's all there is.

When you think like this, you'll realise just how much of the time you're not really there at all. Think about the drive home when you're on autopilot and get there only to realise that you can't remember a single part of the journey. Think about all the days at work where you leave the office not really sure about what you've actually done that day.

The advice to take a conscious decision to live in the moment is probably the single most important piece of business wisdom I have ever received. It means that you can live the dream rather than just dream it. It enables you to learn from the past rather to stay there.

When you manage other people of course, their time takes on a whole new dimension for you too. It's the way that they use, or abuse, their time, which has the greatest potential to make you rich or poor. People, and their time, are almost every company's biggest overhead, and yet most leaders still seem to fail to take them seriously enough. To make the most of your team's time now, consider getting them to record, in blocks of time, what they did with each block, and whether they consider each block to have been used productively, usefully or unproductively. What do you think this would say? Doing this is a big step towards eliminating the negative and accentuating the productive.

Now is always urgent.

TIP 9

KEEP THE FAITH

Big shots are only little shots who keep shooting.

Christopher Morley

W e are living through a global pandemic. No, not flu – this is a pandemic of pessimism.

With so much doom and gloom about, you'd be easily for-given for giving up and going home. When times are hard, and you can't even remember what soft felt like any more, when you've knocked on a hundred doors and not got one positive response, it's easy to think that you're the problem. We've all been there.

But it's not that simple. You need fighting spirit. Those who survive will be the people who realise that necessity is the mother of invention. The people who go the extra mile. Be a seeker, not a sleeper; a doer, not a thinker. If you're facing a challenge that gets your adrenaline flowing you're very lucky: this is the stuff of life.

Keeping faith with your instinct and believing what your gut tells you are what will really set you apart. Remember that the definition of discovery is to have seen the same scene as hundreds or thousands of other people, but to see a different picture. Those who don't see your picture are always going to question you, but it doesn't mean that you're necessarily wrong. Not in the slightest. Remember that it took over 250 pitches to get the start-up funding for Starbucks. Where did all the venture capitalists think they were going to get their soya lattes and frappucinos? J. K. Rowling suffered rejection from nearly every major publisher, before Bloomsbury finally laughed all the way to the bank by signing the *Harry Potter* series. There are countless other stories like these. Dance, and if your idea has legs, the world will eventually dance with you. The motto is: keep believing.

Remember too, however, that like all Big Ideas, keeping the faith should come with a pinch of salt. Not salt, of course, but humility. So long as you're humble enough to listen and to realise how insignificant you really are, you'll guard against the arrogance which could keep you from your aspirations.

When you feel lost and bewildered, remember that everyone else successful has made this very same journey. It's a good discipline to ask yourself what you'd do if you didn't feel so scared. Then do it. You can play safe later; it's far too risky to do so now.

TIP 10

PATIENCE IS A VIRTUE

He that can have patience can have what he will.

Benjamin Franklin

As a virtue, patience is grossly underrated in modern business.

Even if you're able to make cuts and changes quickly and wisely, the effects may take a while to show up in the bottom line of your accounts. Your problems aren't going to come right tomorrow. It's going to be a long, slow haul.

The big decisions that you lose sleep over now may take a long time to come to fruition, and you'll face many more agonising days and nights before you'll know if you've made the right call.

So when austerity conditions abound, and the pressure to operate more efficiently bears down more heavily, you need to make sure you temper any impatience for immediate results with a level head. It is essential to remain patient and to keep your eyes forward, looking up to the horizon and the need to still be strong tomorrow, and not allow yourself to become all consumed by the clear and present dangers.

The pressure is always for the numbers to look good more quickly than is healthy, and to be bank friendly too soon. Shareholders and funders therefore have a tendency to be impatient. As a boss, you need to know when not to listen to all these voices. If all you measure is what's happening here and now, you won't be making the right decisions. More often than not, particularly in a fast-moving, corporate environment, it will even be your successor who will get all the credit. That's life.

When the going gets tough, the toughest develop the patience of a saint.

TIP 11

A COACH IN YOUR POCKET

If I want to be great I have to win the victory over myself ... self-discipline.

Harry S. Truman

Coaching has been fashionable in business circles and beyond for most of the last decade. Coaches can help you discover your goals, aid you in seeing the wood from the trees, help you move on to the next stage, remove obstacles, and supercharge your performance – at least according to all the glossy brochures they will. But austerity business may well allow neither the time nor the money for hours spent in a room with a highly paid outsider talking about your personality. What is an aspiring leader to do?

I use a pocket coach. It's smaller and cheaper. In my wallet, I carry a card that carries my lifetime goals, as well as the top five targets I want to achieve in the next hundred days. What are they? I'm not telling. The point is that I see it every time my wallet is opened. Every time I sit down to work, I place it on my laptop or the desk beside me.

It sounds simple, and it is. It's an elementary discipline that makes a huge difference. When the big objectives you want to achieve are out of sight, they're also out of mind, and it's far too easy to get bogged down in the minutiae. It's an easy way to keep your ambitions real and present, and to bridge the gap between your thinking and your behaviour. Other people do so often get in the way of these, so it's important that you remain focused.

The point about your pocket coach is that it's an amazingly far-sighted little piece of cardboard. While you're panicking about that days sales, or worrying that the team doesn't respect you that week, the pocket coach will help you rise above it all. If you do this for several years, as I've done, you'll realise that the big goals, the things you really want to achieve, will remain the same come rain or shine, whether you're going through austerity or prosperity. This is truly invaluable. Looking beyond your current situation to your next moves works in chess and snooker, and it works in business too.

I promise you that the discipline and focus that your pocket coach will bring will allow you to look forward, and to turn every crisis into an opportunity. These are the true hallmarks of an enterprising person.

TIP 12

KEEP FIT

Lack of activity destroys the good condition of every human being, while movement and methodical physical exercise save it and preserve it.

Plato

Austerity may leave you feeling worn out, helpless and exhausted. When everything seems grim around you, the last thing you will want to do is steam some vegetables before heading out to the gym. In hard times, we all order more pizza, crave a glass of wine to relax, curl up in front of the TV with a big bar of chocolate, or reach for the foods that remind us of our childhood – that's why sales of Arctic Rolls are booming.

You might also suffer from the cult of 'presenteeism' – the feeling that if you're not getting the results you want, at least if you're burning the midnight oil in the office the people around you will see that you're doing something.

I don't want to lecture you, but it's true that staying physically and mentally healthy is the only way to generate the energy you need to keep on keeping on. Show me an unhealthy yet successful business leader, and I'll show you someone who is either lucky, or privileged.

It takes energy to go once more into the breach, energy to be a leader that people want to follow, even more energy to take on the energy sappers and bureaucrats who stand in your way. Health and fitness is the only way that you'll get all of this energy.

Above all, you need mental fitness not to buckle under all this pressure. There are many ways of achieving this, whether it's time spent with family or relaxing in the garden, but here are a few of my favourites.

- No shame in a laugh – If you're not laughing at yourself or your situation pretty much every day the chances are that you're not coping very well either. The best offices are like laughter kegs waiting to burst at any moment. No-one wants to work somewhere that you could cut the silence with a knife. Far too many people mistake being serious with being boring. If anything, you need more laughs when times are tough.

- Meditate – We all need moments when we can switch off completely. Meditation is the best 'off' switch I know. The returns in well-being and productivity of 10 minutes of complete shutdown every day will far outweigh any opportunity cost.

- Embrace serendipity – Think of your journey as a ramble across uncharted territory, rather than a train going down the tracks. Even though austerity is likely to sound the final death-knell for such cosy ideas as a job for life, it's too easy to get stuck on one route and never get off. Instead, you need to bump into people you shouldn't meet and take an interest in new things. Survival will become all about fusion

– fusion of new ideas, practises and cultures. Don't confuse being focused with being blinkered.

- Read, read, read – Knowledge and learning will make a huge difference to your ability to seize the opportunities to see you through austerity. For the price of a few books, you could see the world in a whole different way. Ask the people you respect for their advice on the books that changed the way they saw business. For starters, I'd say that if you haven't read *Who Moved My Cheese*, *The E Myth* and *Good to Great* – you need to pick one and order it now. You can look for inspiration in the words of Winston Churchill or Martin Luther King or the poetry of Rudyard Kipling. What have you got to lose?

- Lose the fear – Make sure that what you're fighting for is worth fighting for. Is it really worth it? Does it put a fire in your belly? If not, you need to change something. You'd soon put down a boring book, or switch from a rubbish TV show, so why carry on doing a job that bores you to tears?

In the end, your success always starts and ends with you.

PART II

PEOPLE

TIP 13

MUSKETEERS AND MERCENARIES

We must all hang together, or assuredly, we shall all hang separately.

Benjamin Franklin

You'll find that leading a team through austerity and adversity shows what the people around you are really made of. You may well discover that your team is determined, glued together by the strong adhesives of trust, respect and fairness, a true band of musketeers. These will be the people who, faced with a crisis, will push that bit harder as a unit, who will offer blood, sweat and tears to see things through.

On the other hand, you may well find that you are surrounded by a collection of hired guns, wedded only to their pay cheques and benefits packages, utterly lacking in that vital esprit de corps. These are the mercenaries, only in it for what they can get for themselves. Whilst the musketeers are staying late, the mercenaries will be away on a last-minute holiday that week.

Anyway, the point of this is that the fact that a crisis shows things in so clear a light, gives you the permission to take unprecedentedly bold decisions. You'll almost certainly find that you don't need the mercenaries and consultants hanging around. Similarly, you'll be likely to value those true musketeers more than ever. You may well have to call on their goodwill, their patience and their perseverance, but the shared experience should bind you all together even more strongly.

In the aftermath of a global crisis, attitudes to work change dramatically. Where once the focus was on career progression, now the humbler ambition of job security comes to the fore. Most people realise that jumping ship in turbulent economic times is the surest way to perish in stormy seas. Even if they wanted to jump, the likelihood is that there will be nowhere to go. In truth, economic austerity will actually mean that most people still in work are better off than they were before. Prices tend to fall quite dramatically, whereas incomes head south more slowly. Despite this, general fear and uncertainty over unemployment will temper behaviour.

Not long ago, the prospect of discussing a whole company pay cut with a trimmed down team would have seemed unimaginable. The fact that this very proposal was accepted by my own team with a sense of relief is an indicator of just how much things have changed. On a larger scale, global consulting firms like KPMG have offered a four-day week to trim costs and avoid laying off unnecessary upturn talent. Equally, BT has been encouraging the outward secondment of staff, whilst picking up 50% of their wage bills.

For those staff, whether mercenaries or musketeers, who've been wanting to take their feet off the pedals by trying something different, be it a new industry, or trekking in Patagonia, austerity can present a golden opportunity. It's far too easy to spend a life climbing up a greasy career ladder, only to find that the ladder was leaning against the wrong wall all the time. Before you go any further: do you think your ladder is up against the right wall?

Whatever you decide, or is decided for you, during the coming period of austerity, it's going to be important to think and act like a musketeer. All for one and one for all! Or, as JFK might have said, 'Ask not what your company can do for you …'.

TIP 14

FOLLOW THE LEADER

If I have seen farther than others, it is because I was standing on the shoulders of giants.

Isaac Newton

Austerity gives all business leaders the permission to act decisively. Anxiety opens up the ears. The people around you are going to want a real leader, not just a manager, and there's nothing like a crisis to sort your Churchill from your Chamberlains.

The importance of leadership spans all fields of human endeavour, from religion to sport, from politics to business. After so much of it, throughout so many centuries, you'd think we might by now actually be able to agree on what it is. But you'd be wrong. A great many rainforests have been chopped down to fuel the debate on what really makes a good leader. Are they born or are they bred? Is leadership a part of good management, or is it the other way around?

Thankfully, at the coalface during austere times, you don't have the luxury of sitting around thinking about the finer points of leadership theory. You have to get on with the job and do whatever you think is right; playing your hand to maximum effect.

In the search for leaders, I always remember the advice of my wise old economics professor that the way to spot a leader is to look for their followers – the leader won't be too far ahead. It's that simple. Leaders in tough times are the ones who are out there, trying new things, setting new standards, and who cajole, inspire and manipulate others to follow suit. Leaders paint a picture of the world, in stark, black and white terms, and get other people to act based on that.

Think about some of the great leaders in history. What sort of performance appraisal forms did Gandhi fill in? Was Mandela that concerned about breaching health and safety guidelines? Leaders just get out there and do the job.

Management, on the other hand is a far subtler, more complex beast. If leadership is black and white, management happens in shades of grey. Management is the murky world of KPIs, lean manufacturing and health and safety. Of course, all that's important too, but tough times call for tough leaders.

Of course, leaders aren't gods, they're not perfect. Even the best of them can't prevent bad things happening. Despite how much is talked about motivation, even the best of leaders can't motivate lazy or disinterested people. Motivation comes from within. All the leader can do is inspire good people to greater things. What distinguishes the best leaders, however, is an ability to admit their mistakes on the run, and be resilient, responsive and flexible.

So, if you're an austerity leader, how will you spot your followers? In my experience, followers divide into five groups.

Knowing this, and working with each group as you find it, can be the key to success.

First, there are the self-starters. These people are like gold dust in any business environment, they only become more precious during times of austerity. These are the people who'll bravely go ahead and do the right thing, even without a leader, although they're glad to have someone else with them on their journey.

Next, there are the hesitant followers. These are people who needed the map, they're neither cartographers nor sherpas, but once they have someone showing the way, they're happy to come along.

Then, there are the determined sceptics. The sceptic will come along with the leader on the journey, but resist and question what they're doing every single step of the way. I've learned never to underestimate the value to a team of a loyal sceptic. That kind of relentless questioning can often rescue a leader from the brink of catastrophe at the last moment.

Never, however, confuse the hesitant and the sceptical followers with the last two groups, the reluctant followers and the cynics.

The reluctant follower would really rather not move thank you, not when staying still is so much more comfortable. Even if forced to, they'll only come along dragging their feet. The cynics are one stage worse. They're not simply lazy, they're a malignant force; they'll always see the problems, but never the answers. Any new ideas immediately get filed in the 'told you so' box. Not only will they not move, they'll try their damndest to stop everyone else coming along too, dragging the whole team down to their level of doubt and torpor.

What to do with these last two groups of followers? For the reluctants, if it becomes a case of 'can't change, won't change', they've got to go. As far as I can tell, cynics never change, so jettison them now before they cost you and everyone else too much time, money and energy.

So there you have it. Be resolute! Kill the pessimists and cynics!

TIP 15

ABOLISH SLAVERY

The people and circumstances around me do not make me what I am, they reveal who I am.

Laura Schlessinger

Abolish slavery? That happened two centuries ago, I hear you say.

But look at it this way, how many times have you heard the phrase 'our people are our greatest asset' spouted by managers and gurus, or wasting space on the pages of corporate mission statements? How many times have you sighed inwardly at the complete pointlessness of it? Along with 'there's no "I" in team' it deserves pride of place in the lexicon of meaningless business English.

The problem with the whole 'our people are our greatest assets' theory lies in the little-noticed fact that companies don't actually own their people. They just rent them. Unless, of course, you're a plantation owner in 18th century America. Didn't think so.

Whether you own an asset fundamentally alters your approach to investing in it. Would you install a new kitchen in a rented flat with a six-month lease on it? Probably not. In the same way, no business can afford to invest mindlessly in the people assets it employs. The employer who does so is deluded – the capital appreciation will all accrue to the employee.

This is, I know, a somewhat controversial view. In delivering it at skills training conferences, I have even been heckled by the audience for suggesting it to be true. Yet the audience always seems less bullish when I asked how happy they would be to find their cleaner or gardener reading up on new cleaning methods or the niceties of horticulture, still surrounded by piles of dirty laundry or an unkempt lawn.

The contract between employer and employee is a very complex one; I won't explain all the ins and outs of it here. I just want to make the point that the best people to have around you in austere times are the ones who invest in their own human capital, rather than expecting to have it all handed to them on a plate. The best people want to improve, practise what they do and love being thrown in at the deep end.

Your people are not your greatest assets, but they will make or break your dreams. The passions you instil and the training you insist upon will determine your prospects for years to come. While you don't own your people, you do own the team, the way it plays and the results you get at the end of the day. This is where your investment should be targeted.

Austerity shouldn't stop you spending on training, far from it. Just do it wisely. Training needs to benefit the team, not just the individual.

TIP 16

IT'S GOOD TO WORK

The best way to appreciate your job is to imagine yourself without one.

Oscar Wilde

These days, it seems like everyone's talking about work–life balance. But in the whole debate, what most fail to realise is that the work slice of the pie has to be bigger than they think, in order to live a life well-spent.

Work is the way that most of us make a difference in the world. At its best, it allows us to realise our dreams, gives us opportunities and allows us to develop. It's not, as some well-meaning pressure groups would have it, an unpleasant inconvenience, a barrier to what would otherwise be an idyllic life of copious consumption and idyllic relaxation. In austere times, there's nothing like a little bit of good, old-fashioned hard work. As a business leader, you have absolutely no reason to apologise for encouraging more of it from your team.

We in Europe have become used to blaming work, or rather too much of it, for all society's ills. Work, we are told, keeps fathers from their children, rips mothers out of the family home and has turned us into a continent of Crackberry addicted zombies. Flexible hours and health and safety have become the order of the day.

With luck, in our more frugal future, the winds may change. When the economically eager workers of China and India seem ready to work round the clock for very little, something has to shake us out of this slumber. In a world of austerity, we must all realise that we are not owed choices that we are not prepared to earn. In truth, work and life are the same thing, they can't be balanced off against each other like the opposite sides of scales. We need to stand full-square against the continual devaluation of endeavour, sweat and what my Granny used to call 'elbow grease'.

Business leaders need to set an example. Avoid burnout, but try your hardest and give it your all. Surround yourself with people like you, who *like* work, who understand how rewarding it can be, and who want to give it their all too. I said austerity was going to be hard, and it will call for hard work. A strong work ethic will serve you well in the times to come. I promise you'll reap the rewards.

TIP 17

DON'T HIRE AND HOPE

People are like stained-glass windows. They sparkle and shine when the sun is out, but when the darkness sets in, their beauty is only revealed if there is a light from within.

Elisabeth Kübler-Ross

Recruiting is a funny business. Given that getting the right people on board is one of the most critical factors for any company's success or failure, it never ceases to amaze me just how hit and miss we are prepared to be about the decision-making process.

We draft a quick advert on the run, glance through a pile of CVs hoping to separate fact from fiction, and then bring a few candidates into the office for a 30-minute chat. After that, if we come away with a vague notion that their face would 'fit', we may carry out a brief reference check, in the certain knowledge that not many former employers would tell us anything that isn't completely anodyne.

We may do stupid things, like hire the person who wants to be paid a couple of grand less, in blissful ignorance of the many thousands more that they could lose you once in the job. Then they're hired, ready and able to create millions or to damage the reputation of the whole enterprise beyond repair. It's all a bit hire and hope.

The sad truth is that we all like to think that we're such incisive judges of human character, that we'll instinctively make the right decisions anyway. Get real.

We are all guilty of failing to plan our recruitment, and therefore planning to fail. By all means, use your gut instinct, but only once you've gathered all the evidence. Seriously consider using psychometric testing, task observations and even basic intelligence and a decision-making test. This is far too important to leave to luck and chance.

If you're anything like most managers and entrepreneurs, you're probably hanging your head in shame at this point. Guilty as charged.

The upside of austerity is that this is the perfect moment to address those times you decided to hire and hope in the past, and to make sure you've got the best team around you. If there are people on your team who never quite lived up to your expectations, and you know you've got to make cuts, it is the time to make sure that the axe falls on their heads. Brutal, but true.

Excitingly, though, not everyone will have been as canny in the cuts they make as you are going to be. There is now a bigger pool of talent out there than there's been for years. Next time you hire, make sure you take a good, hard look in the cold light of day at everyone who's available, and be determined to only pick the best. You're worth it.

TIP 18

ONE SIZE DOESN'T FIT ALL

The first rule is not to lose. The second rule is not to forget the first rule.

Warren Buffett

Too often in a world of rules and regulations, we assume that one size fits all. It doesn't.

My favourite quotation on this subject comes from Edmund Burke:

> *'Because half a dozen grasshoppers under a fern make the field ring with their importunate chink, whilst thousands of great cattle, reposing beneath the shadow of the British oak, chew the cud and are silent, pray do not imagine that those who make the noise are the only inhabitants of the field.'*

If you're not careful, you can end up focusing on the loud problem staff and customers, ignoring the silent majority who do all the hard work or provide all the profit. Quite frankly, we are not all equal. Rules and policies are there to deal with freeloaders. The rest of the people around you deserve a bit of discretion, in austere times as much as ever.

Getting the most out of people is about inherent fairness, mutual respect and flexibility on both sides. Getting the best out of reluctants and cynics is about applying the rules to get them off the team. If you're spending most of your time dealing with the problem cases, you're doing something very wrong.

As you build a team, you must not lose sight of the individual, their needs, talents and desires. F. W. Taylor, one of the first management thinkers, used to think that people were no more than cogs in a machine, which had to be efficiently and scientifically managed. This might have worked in the age of factory production lines, but it sure as hell doesn't work in the modern knowledge economy.

In the fair, even-handed, individualistic management of the people around you, actions speak louder than words. The Romans understood this, when they used decimation to execute one in ten soldiers during periods of insubordination. Obviously, this wouldn't stand up well in an employment tribunal, but being prepared to throw the odd metaphorical grenade is just as important as all the warm and fuzzy stuff. If someone rolls into the office late every day, tell them clearly, in front of the rest of the team, that it just isn't acceptable. In any case refreshing the bottom 10% of your workforce each year is a solid strategy.

To paraphrase Confucius: 'I hear and I forget. I see and I remember. I experience and I understand'.

Of course, the awkward part is that, because one size doesn't fit all in times of austerity, I can't give you an easy template, a business model that will help you get the best out of all your people, day in, day out. It may all feel a bit too tough and tiring. Just do your best.

TIP 19

MEETING THE CHALLENGE

Meetings are indispensable when you don't want to do anything.

J. K. Galbraith

Everyone who has ever worked in an office would probably agree unanimously that meetings are the biggest waste of time.

I can't be the only one continually surprised at the extent to which everyone is continually tied up in meetings. Not only do meetings eat up time, but we also all hate them. They're boring. Nine times out of ten we'll leave them without having established any solution or way forward. If time and money really are so short, why do we torture ourselves like this?

Either we can't bear the thought of an afternoon without a plate of chocolate biscuits within grabbing distance, or there must be a better reason for wasting hour upon hour just exchanging opinions. It seems strange that an individual employee who takes personal calls or spends the day on Facebook is likely to face disciplinary procedures, but we will merrily waste the man and woman hours of ten of our most highly paid people by allowing them 3 hours to chat in a meeting room. For any Trekkies, in the words of Captain James T. Kirk, 'A meeting is an event where minutes are taken and hours wasted.'

Sure, meetings exist for a purpose – they're just another tool in the bag to help you get the job done. They are there to foster faster and better decisions, improve delivery and to ratchet up everyone's energy. But in the wrong hands, especially when times are tough, they become a lethal weapon.

Here are my tips for running an austere but effective meeting:

- only have the essential people there – don't play politics with who gets to come
- don't give anyone a chair – comfort is the enemy of speed
- be out of there in 30 minutes – if it's longer, it's not a meeting, it's a lesson, a debate, or a party.

Remember that austerity in meetings is likely to lead to far greater prosperity of the business. It's good to talk, but it's better to work.

PART III
CUSTOMERS

TIP 20

GOOD VALUE

The result of a business is a satisfied customer.

Peter Drucker

Everyone's come across the shoddy ways that businesses save money when the going gets tough. Electrical products that use cheaper parts, only just staggering to the end of their warranty cycle. Less cheese on your pizza. Smaller chocolate bars in bigger foil wrappings. Shoddy packaging. Too often businesses take their customers for fools, when they're anything but.

Taking value away from the customer is a dangerous game. When customers feel cheated, which they undoubtedly will when they realise you've made them pay the same for less, they'll lose their trust in you. This always spells trouble.

Nevertheless when times are hard, some bright spark will inevitably come up with the idea that you could save thousands by lowering the spend on what your customer actually receives, usually on the basis that they won't notice the change. But if your customers do come to feel cheated, you can never win back their trust. It is your dishonesty as much as the inferior product which will really get to them.

In an austere trading climate, your customers are likely to become more aware of value, and your competition is likely to get keener. If the customers feel they're being conned, quite frankly, you're doomed.

Never lose sight of the fact that the only reason that your business exists is to provide value for customers. Some of the most successful businesses make a point of reserving a portion of profits in any sale to reinvest in the customer relationship, whether by sending a free gift with the order, or by calling to check that everything is OK. This isn't marketing spend, but if you do it well, the positive word of mouth and strong customer loyalty could be worth thousands.

Never short-change your customers.

SELL YOUR SOCKS OFF

Everyone lives by selling something.

Robert Louis Stevenson

When I'm asked what I do at dinner parties, I always give a simple answer. I say 'I'm in sales'. Not that I'm an entrepreneur, or a director, or anything else. Just sales. The response I get is interesting. People often look embarrassed, or wonder how I've held my own in the conversation up until that point. They nearly always look sorry for me, sorry that I haven't managed to get a 'proper' job by this point in my life.

That sums up the problem quite neatly. We're all so embarrassed by sales that we don't want to admit that we all have to do it, all the time. The society we live in still has an outmoded view that sales is either just wheeling and dealing, or the territory of the washed up lower-middle classes. Think Artful Dodger and Fagin, or Willy Loman in Arthur Miller's *Death of a Salesman*. Hardly the kind of role that you'd aspire to at a school careers evening.

But in times of austerity, we all have to come back to a simple truth of commercial life: not a day passes when we are not selling. No longer can we sit back on our laurels and assume that the money will somehow roll in. Selling an idea to the board. Selling a proposition to a client. Selling yourself to a colleague. Selling a product to your customer. Selling a suggestion to a supplier. Selling your business plan to the bank. Even selling to your reader that it's worth their time reading on. In any business, sales is the bottom line.

Do the people around you think they're selling? Are they proud of it? If not, what do they think they're doing? How are they contributing to making any money? Food for thought.

Of course, the nature of sales is changing, even if it remains as important as ever. The idea of the salesman bamboozling the customer with a barrage of benefits is well and truly over. Today, the savvy salesperson subtly makes it easier to buy a product or a service, which will solve a customer problem. In times of austerity, things are likely to be as tough for your customers as they are for you. Good austerity selling consists of recognising this, capitalising on the strength of your existing relationships, and coming up with a solution which will benefit you both in the long run.

I'm not going to pretend that sales, like everything else, aren't tougher to achieve in a recession. It's much tougher. If it used to take 10 calls to get an appointment, now you might find that it takes 15. It might take double the appointments to get a result. As you probably know, in most businesses, it's the sales at the margin that deliver the profits at the end of the day. For many companies, their net profit comes from the last 10% of their sales. That being the case, although a 10% drop in sales might not seem like the end of the world, it very easily could be if it wiped out your entire net profit.

Even once you've got an interested customer, it's even harder to get them to commit. When cash is tight, people normally trade down. Even those customers who're not actually so financially pressed will be feeling that little bit more frugal, and they'll use their new found austerity advantage to push prices down.

I know this all sounds like scary stuff. In many ways it is. Prolonged austerity is uncharted territory for most of us, and sales people, by their very nature, are better at selling than they are at saving. The key issue is that you need to know all this, and then work that bit harder to overcome it.

As a manager, or entrepreneur, now more than ever you must understand that sales are less a cost or an overhead, than the only hope we've got of working ourselves out of this sorry mess. Don't be stingy about selling.

So, don't just sit there panicking, get out there and sell your socks off!

TIP 22

KEEP ON MARKETING

The story of the human race is the story of men and women selling themselves short.

Abraham Maslow

M arketing. It's both your biggest opportunity and your biggest threat in an economy which has bottomed out. Why so?

Only a fool would indiscriminately slash their marketing spend on the basis of an accounting spreadsheet. But there are plenty of fools out there. Make sure you're not one of them.

By spending on marketing, carefully and wisely, you will give yourself the greatest possible opportunity of getting out and surviving. There's plenty of history to point to which demonstrates the folly of turning off the marketing tap in a crisis. Yet again and again, the people who control the purse-strings see marketing as 'soft' money, and target it as one of the first budgets to get slashed. When the crowd all runs away from promotion, walk carefully and purposefully in the opposite direction. Don't be a sheep. You'll be rewarded by lower costs, a lack of competition and the likelihood of substantial dividends. Maintaining this strong focus, this insistence on not just reaping but also still planting the fruits of the upturn, will position you as an austerity winner.

Customer resistance to change also plummets in tough times – everyone knows we need to try something different. It's manna from heaven if you're building a brand.

Go on, test the water. Try even just a small direct mailing, or issue a couple of local press releases. The risk is low, and you could uncover a wealth of untapped potential. You can afford to fail small and often, and still be pleasantly surprised at the times you do win.

The thing is, too many managers have lost their focus on the basics of marketing. A glamorous and glossy image only masks the reality beneath. Others go wrong when they think it's all about creativity, wonderful strap lines and whizz-bang graphics. Of course, these may well play a part, but the reality of marketing is far more boring and far more central. In the end, it's all about testing, assessing, amending, re-testing, scaling up and then, if you're lucky, taking the money.

Remember this: the opportunity cost of not following your good ideas is much greater than giving them a go.

It's true that the days when customers' eyes were bigger than their shopping trolleys has long since passed. When budgets were big, marketing got sloppy. It seemed so much easier to broadcast messages to markets that really needed a narrow-cast, rifle shot approach. Today, with marketing as with so much else, less is usually more. Targeted, measurable, effective activities are where it's at. Be smarter, not cheaper. Define the customers you want, and get out there to hunt them down.

Of course, the very best marketing is based on a close understanding of what customers need. How do you know that? By getting out there and talking to them. Hard times can make you scared, making it easy to hunker down and forget about the world outside. Do this at your peril. Get out there and walk alongside your customers, get to know and understand them, talk to them and *listen* to what they are saying. Observe what they do. Only then will you be best placed to create the messages that tell them what they want to hear, and deliver what they want to get.

When, faced with adversity, the unwise cut their marketing budgets, this tells you that they don't understand their business is founded entirely on customer relationships. Such a knee-jerk reaction is the surest sign of panic, supine leadership and weak management. Austerity isn't all about cutting; it's about spending and saving wisely. You won't save your way out of a tight spot if the savings you make cut off your customers.

I'd go as far as to say that marketing was designed for recessions; that it only truly comes into its own in the jaws of adversity. In the glory days you should do it well, but in the bad times you absolutely must.

PRICE FOR VICTORY

Every man has his price.

Robert Walpole

I t's been more than 200 years since Walpole said this, so you'd think that by now, after generations of practice, we'd have mastered the dark art of pricing. In times of austerity price matters more than ever, so it's a pity that we haven't. In my experience, prices are generally set by amateurish guesswork rather than by hard science. Now, more than ever, it's time to take a long, hard look at how you set your prices.

What is the right price for your product? Do you have any idea? How thoroughly have you checked? What would your profits be like if you thought differently? If pricing is an annual 'finger in the air' exercise, with a cursory look around at the competition, you could soon find yourself in deep trouble. Similarly, if you've got an amateurish 'cost plus target margin' approach you could soon be in for some nasty surprises.

Today's most successful companies, the ones that seem to be hardening and refining their propositions in these tough times – you know them, Google, Dell, Nike, IKEA – all offer crystal clear propositions, with their pricing policies at the very centre of what they do.

The point about price is that it is your mechanism for capturing your share of the value in each transaction. A shocking truth is that many, many people might have been willing to pay you more, sometimes a lot more. In times of austerity, capturing all the available value has never been more important.

This might sound ridiculous. Only in a Monty Python sketch will customers ever ask to pay extra: 'What, £50? I'd gladly pay £60!' If you're waiting for your sales team to put in for higher prices, you may well have to wait some time.

In economic terms, however, the price is simply the level at which consumption will take place between two willing parties. Like so much else, it really is that simple.

Yet it's also a highly sensitive issue. Your customers may well get up in arms about the slightest increase, and the media portray utilities companies which raise prices as little better than robber barons. Yet normally, a higher price indicates a superior solution. Think the iPod against all the cheaper MP3 players out there. On more than one occasion, in my own business, I've found that raising a price has actually increased sales volumes.

We also all have pricing blindspots, where a significant change in either direction won't register. Very few buyers, for instance, even in these straitened times, really notice paying £4.99 rather than £3.99 for the same product, but almost all will see it in your shipping charges. All customers seek value, not just the cheapest thing on the market. Price is a proxy for value, so be sure your customers understand they're getting a good deal.

The key to effective pricing is to take it very seriously indeed, and to give it the time it deserves. The best prices are fair, credible and clear. Keep your prices easy to find, easy to read and reflective of your position in the market.

Make sure your customers don't end up knowing the price of everything you do and the value of nothing.

CARE FOR YOUR CUSTOMERS

Your most unhappy customers are your greatest sources of learning.

Bill Gates

W e've all got them. Actually, we've probably all got lots. I'm talking about those customer service horror stories we all like to trot out over a coffee or down the pub, invariably to the horror and amazement of the assembled company. You know what I mean: the insufferably rude sales assistant; the incompetent call centre; and on and on and on. Almost all of these horror stories are caused by the vast mismatch between loud marketing rhetoric and the ghastly reality – the poor investments in the people and systems needed to deliver on the promises made.

Of course, there are two sides to every story of bad customer service. As you probably know all too well, the customer isn't always right. But it's worth remembering that the majority of gripes are rooted in truth, and that in a world where word of mouth matters, it's what your customers come away thinking that really counts. On the other hand, don't be a customer slave either. Some customers are just angry at life – as a business on the end of this, you just need to absorb their punches and then move on. Don't waste your time running around after the 1% of energy-sapping customers, and ignoring the silent majority who generate your profits.

It's easy, far too easy, for any business to over-promise and under-deliver. We're all guilty of it, especially when customers are raising their demands as they feel the pinch, look for a deal, or play companies off against each other.

The reality is, though, that if your business is perceived as having poor customer service, after a while, you won't have any customers to serve at all, unless you're Ryanair – which is the exception that proves the rule.

Here are a few customer service crimes. Naturally, we should all understand what's so wrong with them by now, but sadly we don't. Perhaps a dose of austerity might just force a few more managers and business owners see the light of day.

- When customers phone your business, they probably want to speak to a person. Don't greet them with an impenetrable, faceless, voice-operated phone labyrinth instead.
- Most of your customers aren't criminals. If, like some train companies, you treat them as if they are, you're only likely to make them very angry.
- Customers want their problems to be solved. That means that it's incredibly frustrating when the person on the other end of a phone line, or service desk, doesn't actually have the

knowledge or authority to do anything about anything, and can only pass the customer on to another faceless cog in the impenetrable system.

If it would annoy you, don't do it to your customers.

TIP 25

WORD OF MOUTH AND MOUSE

While it may be true that the best advertising is word-of-mouth, never lose sight of the fact it also can be the worst advertising.

Jef I. Richards

Y ou've heard it before, but it's worth saying again: *word of mouth matters.*

When Dominos Pizza (a business which has done far better out of austerity than most) launched in the UK, they offered a free pizza for any one delivered outside their 30-minute target. I still remember telling friends 'you won't believe it, they were only a minute late but still delivered us a free pizza'. It was years later before I discovered that the delay was deliberate, conceived to make sure this word of mouth happened as a cheap and effective way of promoting the business. Just by bringing us a free pizza, they encouraged us to do all their marketing for them; they knew what they wanted us to say, and they set it all up for us to say it. It's cheap, and it works wonders. In a world with more and more choice, people rely on their friends, family and neighbours for trustworthy advice about consumer decisions.

When it's done well, positive word of mouth can work wonders for profits by offering up such a low cost of sale. This makes it look easy, which it most definitely isn't. People rarely recite the contents of your latest email blast or leaflet verbatim down the pub with their friends. What gets passed on are stories that are funny, surprising, shocking or thought-provoking: the stuff that engages us emotionally, the stuff that will actually interest our friends.

Manners make the kind of customer service that really gets people talking. Your grandmother may have told you that good manners cost nothing, but when it comes to customer service, that's not strictly true. Getting the right people on board, training them brilliantly and having the management nous to insist on high standards and doing a job that you're proud of, isn't cheap or easy. But it's a whole lot cheaper than the alternative. Make sure your staff say 'please' and 'thank you' and mean it. Don't be patronising – too much 'sir and madaming' annoys everyone, but treat them as equals. Treat them as you'd want to be treated.

Even with limited resources, think of it this way – is there someone in your marketing team dedicated to influencing, checking and making the most of what your customers are saying about you? It's cheaper than most PR, it beats celebrity endorsements and it's less work than winning awards.

With blogs, BlackBerrys and 24-hour news channels bombarding us with information and demanding our attention all the time, it's getting harder and harder to make an impact in these ways; but when you do it, it's magic. In fact, it's amusing to think that word of mouth is now gaining the status of

Killer Marketing App, as a result of the emergence of Twitter, Facebook and LinkedIn. In fact, it's always been the bedrock of all trade; even Egyptian cotton traders knew that centuries ago. *Plus ça change.*

TIP 26

GET YOURSELF
CONNECTED

The Internet is becoming the town square for the global village of tomorrow.

Bill Gates

What! You're not actively re-calibrating your trigger emails with your offline data stream in real time?! It's a wonder you're still trading at all! Where have you been?

I'm joking.

Most of us are spending vast amounts of our limited time and resources in search of gold online. Hardly a day goes by when we are not all snow-flaked with the latest wheeze about how to be number one on Google's page rankings. A whole new language of analytics, affiliates and usability has taken over from the basic stuff we used to all understand, like price, margin, volume and sales. So many managers and entrepreneurs are lost in a complex matrix of technological advance and societal change and they are paralysed by fear. Stop. Fear and panic won't get you anywhere.

Of course, the Internet matters. For the past decade it's been an enormously powerful way of finding new customers, products and suppliers, and a boon to businesses everywhere. But when resources are limited, getting too caught up in it could be fatal by causing you to take your eye off the ball. Don't run around online like a headless chicken. All new technologies cause fear and paranoia. It's hard to separate the gold from the emperor's new clothes in the online world. No-one wants to miss the killer app. But it's alright to calm down a bit and not be worried that you're not best mates with Stephen Fry on Twitter.

Stay focused on what you want from the Internet, rather than what you think it's demanding of you. You can't control technological change, but you can control your reaction to it. Do what works, do what makes sense and what your customers will understand. Find them where you know they'll be looking, and the rest will fall into place.

TIP 27

FORGET OUT-OF-FOCUS GROUPS

If I'd asked customers what they wanted,
they'd have said a faster horse.

Henry Ford

Think back to the mid-1990s. It seems like a long time ago, doesn't it? Apart from that, who among your friends was saying that they really wished they could carry around all their music in something the size of a cigarette lighter, which also held all their photos and doubled as a video recorder? Probably none of them. But that doesn't mean they don't all have iPods and iPhones and iWhatever else now.

Focus groups are expensive bear-traps. The best businesses aren't customer led, they're behaviour led. They create something, using gut instinct, creativity and fire in their belly, that people both need and find they want.

The good news for austerity business is that it can be cheaper to do things this way. The bad news is that it's almost always much harder to identify winning ideas, and requires real talent and nous.

The weakness in looking to your customers to bring you new ideas, is that their experience revolves around what you already do, so the best you can hope for is ideas for a tweak here or a different finish there. Nobody wandering down the High Street would have suggested Starbucks or Macdonald's before they came along.

So many businesses stumble and falter when it comes to innovation. One of the biggest lessons you can learn about this is that the best new ideas often come from your team. I'm not suggesting a suggestion box, just that getting out there and talking to the people you work for can be a very cheap way indeed of researching new ideas.

Another trick of developing innovation that actually ships, is to get beyond what the customer consciously thinks by taking a careful look at how they actually behave. What we all say to one another is very often at odds with our behaviour, so it's important to get to the real behaviour and motivation beyond the words. I might say that I'd prefer a cheaper Porsche, yet much of the cache that makes a Porsche interesting revolves around the fact that it's so expensive that not everyone can afford it. If it were cheap and everyone had one, I'd probably buy an Audi. I might say I want you to be more environmentally friendly by using re-usable packaging, but if it means sharing higher costs, most customers will be unhappy.

One way of getting round this problem of finding out what your customer *really* wants is to test them without letting them know they're being your guinea pigs. For example, we all complain about junk mail these days, but we still like getting cards and letters in the post – a birthday e-card from a friend still feels like a bit of an insult. Rather than yet another impersonal mass mailing, why not try handwritten, personalised cards to key customers, referring them to your website, and see what happens?

Nobody likes to be treated as a number or part of a group; the best innovations treat customers as the individuals they are.

ON WITH THE SHOW

I never call my work an 'art'. It's part of show business, the business of building entertainment.

Walt Disney

Business is like the theatre. It's about creating a storyline, an illusion that draws your customers in, putting your best foot forward. The idea of business as theatre captures some of the energy and drama of day-to-day life in most businesses.

Whether it's the way you light a restaurant to achieve the right effect, or the impact on customers who open a package you've shipped, it pays to think about the effect that you're creating. Like a duck, it doesn't matter if your legs are working frantically below the surface; what matters is looking like you're gliding majestically on top of the water.

We need to pay increasing attention to the theatre of what we do, the show, while all the time keeping the bits the customer isn't supposed to see, well hidden. You don't want customers on your booth the day before the trade show begins when you're in a mess, guests using the scruffy service lifts in your hotel or shoppers in the 'Goods-in' bay in your store.

What does your packaging say? Do the people who deliver your parcels convey the kind of image you want? Do you have the right level of mystique? Does the lighting in your shop make people want to spend time there?

In thinking about business as show time, don't rely too much on customer satisfaction surveys. They're far too after the fact, and they rely on what your customers think good should look like, not what you know it to be. Mystery shopping works far better as an indicator of what it's really like to be a customer. At an even more basic level, have you ever mystery shopped your website? An hour spent online as a customer could be one of the most valuable hours you ever spend.

Of course, business as showbiz isn't about being perfect, just the need to look confident and like you know what you're doing.

TIP 29

YOUR WORD IS YOUR BRAND

He goes by the brand, yet imagines he goes by the flavour.

Mark Twain

I n tough times, reputation is everything.

When the business environment around you switches from plenty to poverty, from disposability to durability, from bling to austerity, your reputation can save or strangle you.

One problem is the word 'brand' itself. It's been so used, overused and abused in the past few decades, that it's really not that useful any more. It's the language of consultants, guff and waffle. You know the kind of thing 'We must remain true to our core strategic values, ensure all stakeholders stick to the branding guidelines, and minimise dilution of our brand equity.' What?

Here's my advice on sounding the jungle drums in tough times – ban the brand and instead rekindle a heartfelt passion for your reputation across your entire team. That's what's really important. Austerity doesn't leave any room for stupid management gobbledegook.

You can't control it, but you can't ignore it either. You can't buy it, you have to earn it. If this all sounds a bit too frightening, the good news is that there are a few focused things that you can do to build your reputation on scarce resources, and turn the way that you are perceived into worthwhile bottom-line benefits.

First, you have to realise how precious and delicate reputation really is. You can spend years diligently building one up, only to have it blown in seconds, by one stupid action, or even through no fault of your own, as often happens to retailers when they are forced to recall a manufacturer's faulty product. Bear that in mind with your reputation – it ought to come in a box marked 'fragile, handle with care'. As Warren Buffett once said: 'It takes 20 years to build a reputation and five minutes to ruin it. If you think about that, you'll do things differently.'

We create our corporate reputations through countless little actions every day. If you're in the habit of paying your suppliers a couple of days late, you'll develop a reputation as a late payer. You may be able to live with that, but few companies would last very long if they got a reputation for paying their staff late.

The second rule of managing your reputation is: don't talk about it. Seriously, it may be useful internally, but your customers really don't care whether or not you are 'dedicated to quality service and customer focus'. Nor are they likely to be interested in the fact that you provide 'excellence through synergy and quality'. They won't even know what 'quality, diversity and integrity means'. Of course, they are interested to hear that John Lewis is 'never knowingly undersold' or that

Tesco thinks 'every little helps', but then that tells them what the company does for them, not what it thinks of itself. With reputations, as with so much else, actions really do speak so much louder than words.

Speaking of actions, the thing here is that you must be clear and consistent. Know how you want to seem, and then be like it all the time. There's a huge temptation to bounce between promotional campaigns, trying to be all things to all people, but it will cost the earth and it won't work.

Sit back and think: 'What should 'made by you' mean? What do you want people to expect from you? What would be out of character? Will you be professional or amateur? Personal or commoditised? Serious or playful? Once you've got it, you need to make sure that everyone else understands it too. Talk to the people in your team about it, make sure that it makes sense.

Then go ahead and be it. Make sure that you answer the phone and march the approach of your delivery drivers to it. Remember all the time you do this that it takes nine good experiences to make up for one negative one.

Just as it takes years to fix a reputation, you can't build one overnight either. Make sure you've got clear, measurable milestones and track them – everyone needs to be accountable for their impact on your reputation.

Although it's not easy, in the age of austerity, the right reputation is worth its weight in gold.

PART IV
STRATEGY

DREDGE THE POND

Keep looking below surface appearances.
Don't shrink from doing so just because you
might not like what you find.

Colin Powell

I n the centre of the village where I live, there's a lovely little duck pond. It's a pretty idyllic scene, surrounded by trees, with daffodils in the spring and lilies in the summer, often with a mother duck followed by a straggle of fluffy yellow ducklings. To all intents and purposes it's the epitome of the English rural idyll.

Yet one summer, it all got a bit unpleasant. We experienced unprecedentedly low rainfall, and an abnormal number of hot, dry days. As the summer went on, the water level dropped, exposing all sorts of unpleasant objects lurking just below the surface. The rusting pushbikes and shopping trolleys came into full view. The fact that they were there at all was a big surprise, but once we had seen them, we couldn't just ignore them. Uncovering the mess compelled us to address the issue, and come to terms with the reality that our picturesque pond hadn't been all that it seemed on the surface.

You may well think that my tranquil village pond is a world away from the rough and tumble of doing business in the age of austerity, but I believe that for most good businesses, the recession has had an effect very similar to the one the drought had on the pond.

The corporate equivalent of dredging the pond means cleaning out all those previously hidden inefficiencies, offloading any marginal or under-utilised personnel and maintaining your assets. We ought to thank the sometimes hysterical media coverage in the early days and weeks of the crisis for scaring us all so witless early on in the cycle. Only being so scared forced us to remove our blinkers, see what we should have been checking for all along, and wade on in there to do the dirty work. As a result, wise businesses shed costs at every corner, shifted marketing spend to focus more on existing customers and better outcomes, and reduced stock levels and working capital needs. This is all good, sensible stuff. It's just a pity that it needed a once in a century shock to the entire capitalist system to get us to do anything about it.

Austerity, at its most useful, exposes the hidden rot. It forces us to see past the grey emptiness of bland corporate missions and values statements to the messy, technicolour reality of what business is really like. Use what may seem like a crisis to clear out the rubbish, spring clean, de-clutter and get ready to push forward all over again.

TIP 31

YOU WON'T SAVE YOUR WAY TO SUCCESS

You have to learn the rules of the game. And then you have to play better than anyone else.

Albert Einstein

I can guarantee you one thing. You won't save your way to success. That might sound a bit odd, in a book about austerity, cutting your cloth and all that.

Of course, I don't mean that you should head out on an enormous spending spree just as the bank cancels your overdraft facility and your hopes of refinancing vanish behind the horizon. By all means, save the pennies by cutting cleverly. Just make sure you're also investing the pounds properly too. Anyone can scrimp and save, but it takes a real entrepreneur to know where to be bearish and where to be bullish when times are tough. Business is about maximising your return on investments, not shrinking.

Saving comes naturally to many entrepreneurs. You may well hate to waste anything, and always attempt to hunt down a bargain. Many of us have been motivated by backgrounds where money was tight. In the early days of a start-up, the 'waste not want not' mentality will serve any business well. But, I'll say it again, businesses don't exist so people can sit in offices concentrating on not spending money. They're there to create value by investing in ideas and opportunities.

Cheapskates don't grow. If you always go for the cheap deal, the cheaper employee and the cheapest suppliers, you may well find that you're not making any money to spend in the not too distant future.

So here are the dos and don'ts of austerity saving without scrimping.

- Do renegotiate with your electricity and printer cartridge suppliers (more competitive rates will almost certainly now be available).
- Do think about whether you really need a new water cooler and luxury biscuits, or whether tap water and digestives might not be good enough after all.
- Do switch the away day for the executive team with a swish hotel to the park.

All that is sensible austerity.

- Don't, however, switch to cheap legal advice without thinking very carefully about what you're doing.
- Don't start pulling the wool by making your products with cheap components, or skimping round the edges of the service you offer to your customers.
- Don't even think about getting your staff to pay for their own coffee – it's just not worth the anger and resentment.

By all means be parsimonious. Cash is, after all, king. This is really just an austerity health-warning. If you're looking down at your cash-flow too much, controlling spending rather than directing investment, you may find that you'll trip up in the long run.

As your grandmother may well have said, penny wise, pound foolish. Cut consumption but increase investment. Simple really.

BREAD TODAY, JAM TOMORROW

The key is not to prioritise what's on your schedule, but to schedule your priorities.

Steven R. Covey

Tough times mean tough priorities.

The first rule of austerity is to know what you're spending. This may sound like the bleeding obvious, but if you talk to many of the entrepreneurs who have fallen on hard times recently, it's truly astonishing how many of them didn't really have a grip on this until it was far too late.

The second rule, then, is to sit down and carefully list your spending priorities. With a limited supply of money, it's essential that you're sure that what you do have is going to all the right places. Having written it all down should mean you're able to see things in the cold light of day.

Do you really need that new company van? Thought not. Will expensive art in the reception area really have an impact on profits? Who are you kidding? Do you need to go to that expensive trade show, or are you just frightened about what your competitors will say when they see you're not there. Could your brochures be just that little bit less glossy?

Where is it that your company really adds value? What makes you stand out? It could be your levels of customer service, the superiority of your product, or the quality of your marketing. There's no universal right answer. Just so long as you know what it is, know why it is, and bear it in mind to prioritise those areas that will feed your growth, all day every day.

Nearly a century ago, Pareto, an Italian economist, came up with what we now call 'the Pareto Principle'. Put very simply, it's the idea that 80% of value comes from 20% of activity. You can see it at work in all areas of business life – your staff, your marketing, your customers, almost anything. In terms of your investment too, it's probably 20% of what you spend that contributes 80% of your profit. The trick is, finding out which is the 20 and which is the 80. Once you've done that, you'll find that a lot of the rest sorts itself.

Austerity means it's imperative to separate those vanity, nice-to-have projects from the real bread-and-butter core of your business – paying your staff, paying your suppliers and just getting on with the basics.

Focusing on bread today, becoming that bit leaner and meaner, will mean you're much more likely to get at that jam, if not tomorrow, then very soon.

TIP 33

WASTE NOT, WANT NOT

Wilful waste makes woeful want.

Scottish proverb

Waste not, want not. One of the oldest austerity sayings, and almost certainly one of the most useful for the modern entrepreneur or business leader.

The thing is, even if the global economy hadn't briefly gone belly up, wasting a little less would do us a lot of good anyway. In the past couple of years, the environment and the economy have come together in a perfect storm, to make us think about our profligacy and change our ways.

But waste has become institutionalised. Everyone else does it, so it's OK, isn't it? It's a rare business that doesn't find ways of cooling profits by pumping money into unnecessary vanity schemes. Times have changed. If you're burning your profits, douse the flames immediately.

Wasting not can be pretty simple. It's often the most boring things that make the biggest difference. Do you still do any of the following:

- leave computers on standby?
- have the office heating on at the weekends?
- use the aircon with the windows open on a warm summer's day?
- leave the office lights on all night?

- print out swathes of paper only to chuck them all in the bin?

If you do, you're hugely out of step with the way the world is going. Austere times just won't allow this kind of behaviour to go unpunished.

The good news, however, is that by taking these little steps you can do your bit for saving the planet, whilst also saving your business. It's an easy win–win.

One of the best ways to cut back on unnecessary waste is to crowdsource your ideas. In managerial positions, it's all too easy to become cushioned from realities of day-to-day expenditure, but you'll find when you ask people on the ground that they really know what's money well spent and what isn't. They'll know that you probably don't need all the daily papers because no-one reads them anyway. They'll tell you what software packages you can get rid of because everyone hates the system and never uses it. They'll also tell you just how damaging it would be to morale to cancel the Christmas party – no-one wants to work for Scrooge. Listen to them.

If you trim that flab now, you'll be surprised at how much you can save.

TIP 34

SECURE YOUR SUPPLY LINES

The amateurs discuss tactics; the professionals discuss logistics.

Napoleon Bonaparte

T he supply chain is the Cinderella of the business world. Every business has one, every business spends a big chunk of their out-goings on it, but no-one really wants to talk about it. It's just too unsexy.

The truth, however, is that it's vastly underrated as a place to save money and extract value. Taking your supply chain for granted has always been an error. It's risky at any time, but in times of economic turmoil, pressure and uncertainty it could be fatal.

Supply chains have always been a difficult balancing act. You can't batter your suppliers to death over price, nor can you enter into happy clappy memoranda of mutual understanding with each other, in the belief that it will mean you do anything useful. In the supply chain, you are the customer. Like any customer, your goal is simple – to get as much sustainable value as possible for your money.

The trick is to align with suppliers who place a low value on what you need most – that's a true win–win. A cash supplier may well be able to meet your need for longer payment terms if you can give them the slightly higher margin they covet.

To really work your supply chain, you must be crystal clear about what you need and expect from the relationship with each and every supplier. You've got to know what you want in order to get it. Then, you must be clear about the possibilities. Put yourself in your supplier's shoes, think about what they value and what you can get out of this. Look around, suss out the competition and see what you could get elsewhere.

Managing your supply chain proactively, rather than sitting back and waiting to be handed a new contract, is the way to win in the supply chain, shaving off cost and increasing your margin.

The chances are that the businesses at every end of your supply spectrum are suffering just as much, if not more, than you are. You don't have to be telepathic to work out what they're thinking.

They're probably downsizing, plugging cash drains, reducing stock, protecting margins and pushing their suppliers for better terms. With so much in flux, glitches are bound to appear – often in the most unexpected places.

What would you do if the weakest link were to suddenly snap? Do you have alternatives lined up, or would you be scrabbling round on the Internet after the fact? Understanding who and what is out there will not only protect you in case of failure; it will also mean that you understand the market better, and will mean you're able to negotiate more sensibly.

You probably feel like you need this extra job like a hole in the head, what with everything else going on right now. But if you're able to do this, and do it well, you're likely to look back on it in calmer times as a seminal moment. You'll thank austerity for it. In my experience, the businesses who understand their supply chains are the businesses that win.

So many companies treat their supplier pool as servants or slaves. How much better could you be though, if you were able to tap into all your suppliers' new products, ideas and approaches? If you treated them as an intelligence circle? The only sustainable relationship you can have with your suppliers is a win–win one, based on mutual benefit.

When you're really talking to your suppliers, they're also much less likely to spring surprises on you. They may well sound you out about that possible price increase, rather than just do it, giving you a chance to negotiate.

Another plus side of sorting out your supply during a time of austerity is that everyone is a lot hungrier for your custom. The major suppliers, who may not have been interested in your volumes, may suddenly now want to listen. For you, that could mean access to a much bigger, more robust and cost-efficient supply base. Pretty tempting.

You can also make the most of your supply chain by hunting like a wolf. You see, the interesting thing about wolves is that they hunt in packs, thereby sharing heat and conserving their stamina as they home in on their prey.

Whilst I'm not suggesting that your suppliers are anything like your prey, hunting in packs for the things you need to procure is no bad idea. When you start to think like this, I promise you, you'll find so many opportunities for innovation.

There are so many chances out there to collaborate with users of other similar services, which we just ignore because we're so busy fending for ourselves. If you think of every single other business as a competitor, you're missing out big time. Could you collaborate with other businesses around you to get better deals on your web suppliers, your ISP providers, your mobile phone suppliers and accountants? These are supplies that I bet you all need. By pooling, sharing and consolidating aspects of your resources and supply chain, you could really cash in. Only your fear of shared action is holding you back.

Why not invest a couple of hours in seeking out ten non-competing businesses with similar needs to yours and getting them to join your pack? Ten phone calls really isn't a huge commitment, and if you could save 10% or more on key costs it would be more than worth it.

Cinderella shall go to the ball, and hopefully save you some money while she's there.

TIP 35

FOCUS, FOCUS, FOCUS

Drive for show, but putt for dough.

Bobby Locke

'm talking about the difference between image and priorities here. What do you need to really focus on to win, and what can be allowed to fall by the wayside? Only by focusing with laser-sharp clarity on your priorities, can you keep your eye on the ball, the only reason you should be bothering at all – to make a profit. As they say in golf: 'drive for show, putt for dough'.

Surrounded by economic detritus, it's easier to say that you should focus on your priorities than to actually know what they now are. I know what you mean. For me, though, the three that you need to prioritise are all fairly obvious. They are:

1   growing the bottom line
2   building your brand
3   improving cash efficiency.

Concentrate here. Test and measure everything you do against these three headline objectives and you won't go too far wrong. This should get you out of a hole and help guarantee your long-term success. Every action you take should be tied to one of these objectives, and preferably at least two. As Gandhi told us, 'Action expresses priorities.'

In business, of course, the reality of your priorities is demonstrated by how you spend your money.

The thing that most people forget is that working capital is finite. It can either be put to work for you short-term and regularly recycled, or locked away in slow-burn, long-term activity. Of course the classic mistake in times of austerity is to hold piles of slow-moving stock, but there's much more to bad practice than that. If you're not looking well ahead into the distance you're probably sacrificing more of your edge than you need to for deeper comfort than is necessary.

Don't hoard cash either. Your granny might have stashed all her money under the mattress, but austerity or not, this is no way to run a 21st century business. Of course, it can make sense to have something squirreled away for the rainy day that cheap assets may become available, but to hoard money, to become terrified of spending anything, just because you're scared and you don't know how bad it's going to get is not a strategy. Cash efficiency is the Ace. Send the money you've got out to work for its living. The best way I know of surviving austerity is to be flexible, nimble and to keep your fixed liquidity needs very low.

Cash-efficient sales are the best ones to make. Of course, they always have been, but it takes a crunch to make us see how important this really is. I know it's the least glamorous end of business, but payment terms really make a bigger difference than you might think. I'm sure you're smart enough to realise that if you take payment at 120 days rather than 90 days, this adds 30 days of finance cost to your bill. But the real cost is not this; it is the opportunity cost of the business you can no longer take on. If you could achieve 30-day collection and re-cycle your cash faster, you would be able to finance four times the level of business, compared to 120-day collection. So you are avoiding four times the turnover and profits. It might be boring, but if you give cash efficiency the attention it deserves, you'll win in the long run.

Driving for show is when you take on the vanity projects. We all know the ones, the big customers who're so expensive to service and deal with that you're unlikely to make any actual money at the end of the day. Most of us have done it too. In times of austerity vanity is a habit that is too expensive to feed.

Think about your customers and how you work with them in the cold, hard light of day. Is that customer really helping your cash-flow, or are they slow payers who tie up much needed resources? Will all your customers help you to meet your long-term goals? These might sound like strange questions to ask, but take my word for it, the ability to discriminate between customers and then to work with the best ones is often what sets businesses that survive aside from those who fall by the wayside.

Of course, the idea of walking away from customers is often a terrifying prospect. You'll worry about the volume you stand to lose, what your competitors might gain by picking up the slack, and that you'll lose economies of scale. In times of austerity, none of these things matter. Focus on cash effectiveness first, long-term profitability second and your reputation always. The rest is a distraction.

What about putting for dough? Quite simply, in the context of business, this means recognising that getting the outcome you need is all that really matters, and focusing on it, directing all your energies and everything you do towards it.

Nobody remembers a great drive if you miss the putt.

TIP 36

ASSUME MAKES AN ASS ...

What gets measured gets done ...

Anon

Knowledge is power.

When times are hard you'd better remember this. When profits are scarce, knowing what's going on will make the difference between winning and losing. You need to know what you're doing.

Even though money might be scarce today, information most certainly isn't. We've got more information at our fingertips than humans have ever had before. Knowing about your customers and your markets used to be pretty hard, a combination of guess work and time-consuming number-crunching. Market research used to be the preserve of the biggest companies with the deepest pockets. Not any more. Now even the smallest of businesses has got access to a world of knowledge, at little or no cost. Use it. There is no excuse for acting on your whims any more – as the old adage goes 'assume makes an ass out of you and me'. Don't think, know.

How many people click through to your marketing emails? Where in the world are the people visiting your website? What are the latest figures from your competitors? If you don't know all this, I suggest you put this book down, and go out there and find out. Make sure it paints an accurate picture too – there's less room for margins for error in austerity conditions.

With all this knowledge, you can be leaner, meaner and more targeted.

Business has changed. You think you can rely on the same old measures as before? Don't believe it. Lazy excuses like 'if it ain't broke don't fix it' or 'don't look too closely' just won't wash any more. Revisit every corner of your business, look at how you measure it and be realistic about whether that's really what you need to know. This is no time for legacy ways of looking at and measuring things.

Once you've decided on the measures you're going to use, you need to get everyone focused on them. Everyone in your team or your company needs to know where the goal is and be shooting at it constantly.

But a word of warning. You can lose as well as win by numbers. That might seem odd, when I've spent most of this book talking about how important it is to watch your cash-flow like a hawk and scan those sales figures with an eagle eye. Yes indeed. But if that were all there is to it, computers would be CEOs by now.

The reason they're not is because, in this austere, changing and highly competitive world, you can't create value by numbers alone. Of course, we all need ways to measure viability, profitability and success. That's where numbers are useful. But we must always remember in doing this, that they should be our servants, never our masters.

Success in business is an art as much as a science. Any manager, leader or entrepreneur who spends large chunks of the day pouring over the latest charts and management models, or refining the business plan or three-year strategy for the nth time, is missing out on perhaps the most crucial aspect of success: the human factor.

Business is about doing, not thinking. Weak leaders think too long and act too late. Don't get dazzled in the headlights of too much information. In these days of balanced scorecards and viral intelligence, analysis paralysis is a very real peril. There's nothing worse than gathering lots of information and then just sitting on it. Even worse is the business leader who gathers reams of data and then spends hours poring over it, while carrying on merrily going about business in exactly the same way as before.

Measure it simply, then do it.

TIP 37

NO SURPRISES

The only thing that should surprise us is that there are still some things that can surprise us.

François de la Rochefoucauld

M ost businesses hate surprises. Small businesses really loathe them and are extra vulnerable to them. We all suffer from myopia and short-termism. When you're flying high and takings are good, it's only human to assume that things will always be like that. That's partly how we got into this mess in the first place.

But if anything's certain about this age of austerity, it's that it's going to be a lot more uncertain.

There's an important distinction to be made here between the 'didn't spot' surprise and the 'couldn't have spotted' one. In the first category, there are things like running out of cash, failing to pay the bills, being burgled with no insurance, etc. Into the second category fall things like economic meltdown, natural disasters and global pandemics. With the first kind, you ought to have known better, and you'll doubtless want to kick yourself over it forever. With the second kind, it's still pretty bad, but if you really have done all you can, at least that's something.

It's ironic, really – not playing safe is the very lifeblood of the entrepreneurial spirit, but it's this very devil-may-care, it-will-all-turn-out-alright in the end attitude which often leads small businesses into trouble, especially in turbulent times.

To avoid this, you need to ask yourself the really tough questions and think about the worst-case scenarios. What would happen if your biggest customer went bust owing you everything? What if the bank got jittery and cut your overdraft facility? What if your biggest supplier changed your terms?

Prepare for each of these scenarios, write down what you'd do and how easy it would be to survive, if at all. Once you know this, it will give you a good, clear sense of how robust you are, what your limitations are, and what you can and can't survive, which should reassure you in even the worst of troubles.

The art of being a successful leader is to shoot hard for the upside, whilst covering off the downside as best you can.

TIP 38

AVOID PERFECTION

Failure is another stepping stone to greatness.

Oprah Winfrey

t's good to fail. This turns most conventional business wisdom on its head, but it really is.

Failure is underrated. It keeps your ego in check if you can learn to lose well and often. Winning teams are more often than not made up of a bunch of losers who've looped through the 'tried, failed and learned' cycle a bit faster and harder than the rest of the pack.

It is the fear of failure that provides the greatest barrier to success. If you're so scared to try a new approach, how will you ever know if it's better or worse? The truth is that there are no failures, just a series of experiences followed by your reaction to them. It is getting stuff wrong that teaches you what you need to know to make it right, so each episode is in fact a step on the road to achievement. It's widely known that Edison tried over 5000 times before he managed to invent the electric light. He was no failure. The only true failure in life is the failure to try.

If you interview someone and they suggest they've never failed at anything in their professional lives, I can guarantee you that they'll either be a liar, or someone who's too scared shitless to try for anything that's worth getting. Keep a wide berth.

The opposite of failure, you see, is perfection. Nobody and nothing has, is or ever will be perfect. Like tomorrow, 'perfect' simply never turns up. For that reason, being angry about not achieving perfection will get you nowhere.

Reserve your anger and frustration for the people who're happy to settle for second-best. Don't expect perfection, but do expect your team to want to improve and win, to believe that even if there's no 'perfect', there's always 'better'. Surround yourself with a team who have it in their blood that everything can be improved upon, people who simply refuse to settle for low standards and who understand the bar is always being raised.

TIP 39

KISS

Simplicity is the ultimate sophistication.

Leonardo da Vinci

This kind of KISSing is anything but romantic. Of course, I mean 'Keep it Simple, Stupid'.

The world is big and confusing enough. We've all got far too much to think about as it is. There are many, many ways to weigh yourself down and make life more difficult than it needs to be. In times of austerity, with so much else to worry about, no-one – not your staff, not your customers, not your suppliers – wants you to make their life one single iota more complicated than it already is.

As humans, we crave simplicity. We like clear messages and easily deciphered patterns to emerge from the chaos of everyday life. The minute you make a subject even the slightest bit complicated, you'll lose half your audience at the drop of a hat.

Think about a PowerPoint presentation. We've all suffered from the infamous 'Death by PowerPoint'. Of course, what really works best, rather than endless graphs and charts, is one simple graphic, or a speaker who's confident enough just to stand and talk to you.

The annoying thing about simplicity, unfortunately, is that it's much more easily said than done. Anyone who writes advertising copy will tell you how hard it is to convey real meaning through just a few words. Get it right, though, and you'll reap the rewards – you'll make your goals so simple that even you can't avoid them any longer; your staff will have no excuse for saying they don't understand; and you'll stick around in your customers' minds.

Simplicity matters as much in your work environment as it does in communication, of course. You'll find that austerity is a tough battle. When you're fighting it, you won't want to be dragging around masses of extra kit that you'll never need. Simplicity is lean and mean. Operate a regular discipline of de-cluttering your workspace, mind, plans and systems. Are you really going to read last year's pile of trade magazines? Really? Bin them (or rather, recycle them – you know, waste not want not and all that).

Simplicity, you see, is like gardening – it requires constant pruning.

INDEX